T0198835

Life's Dream

Changing Love

Robert Rogers

Life's Dream

Changing Love

To order additional copies of this book, contact:
Xlibris
844-714-8691
www.Xlibris.com
Orders@Xlibris.com

ISBN: 979-8-3694-0181-1 (sc)
ISBN: 979-8-3694-0182-8 (e)

Print information available on the last page

Rev. date: 06/23/2023

Contents

A new Destination

I walked through her door
Saw her smile
I'd been gone for awhile
I said "come"
Go with me
A new destination
Let me show you what our love can be
The road is newly paved and straight
Walk with me
Enjoy what you see
We will watch an awaking day
Bask In the rising sunlight
Feel a growing warmth
Wait for the night
Hold each other tight
Our love will burn bright
Kiss
Lasting love is like this
Remember the warming sunlight
Love the night
Share our love in bright sunlight and glowing night

"Yesternight the sun went hence,
And yet is here today"
(John Dunne (1575-1631)

Know our love endures Endless
A caring fulfilling love

Car Wash

She was in the car wash
Fumbling quarters
I stepped toward her
Asked if I could help
She handed me the change
She pressed the handle
Aimed at that '85 Chevy
Drenched herself in soap
Didn't know what to do
Rinse?
Those jeans hung tight
What a sexy sight
I pulled my hands down her legs
Her eyes were bright
She stood still
Wondered what would reveal
I could feel what was real
I said let's park that Chevy in a dry place
Let me take you home
She was wet but I didn't care
I liked her that way
She smiled and said OK
She opened the house door
Said would you like to feel more
I didn't know what to say
Didn't know she felt that way
A car wash can be an interesting place
I will go again

"I love the idea of there being
Two sexes, don't you?"
(Thurber (1894-1961)

2

Dreams Linger

My life is strange
I wish it could be rearranged
It moved in unexpected ways
Sometimes predictable Sometimes not
I remember when I was young
Knew not what I would become
Wanted to fulfill my dream
Dreams are fragments in the night
I still see him
It seems real
When I'm awake that's still how I feel
I hunger
War is heartbreaking
He once was with me
My life glowed
He will never come back to me
War ended my burning plea
He lives only in my dreams
I live in sorrowfulness
It endures with me
The dream lingers

"The joy of love is too short. . ."
(Charles Orl'eans (1391-1465)

3

Everlasting Memories

My memories are everlasting
Nothing will change them
They will forever survive
I will always remember the past
You possess my fondest dreams
They remind me of you
They won 't come true
I keep the memories alive
A bit unwise
I know you will not return
But I still yearn
I am foolish
I cannot forget the hunger
The wild laughter

The music
The dance
The outcomes we left to chance
Our love was linked in pieces
It broke apart
Never join again
I can't relive the past
The laughter
The music The dance
But I will forever remember

"What peaceful hours I once enjoyed
How sweet their memory still!
But they have left an aching void. . ."
(Cowper (1731-1800)

Feel The Warmth

She was sleeping
I could hear her heart beating
I remember it well
It combined with mine
When she woke, I held her close
It was a wonderous time
The sun began to rise
Her eyes met mine
She was not surprised
I could see the glow in her eyes
She said let's stay here for awhile
Watch the sun rise
Feel the warmth
It was welcomed
The sun sometimes fails to shire

She is no longer mine
Why I don't know
We seemed to love each other so
Love can be fleeting
It may only remain for awhile
The sun sets
The warmth fades
Only the memory remains
Let us savor the sun
Celebrate the warm rain
Let warm love remain

"Love comforteth like sunshine after rain"
(Shakespeare)

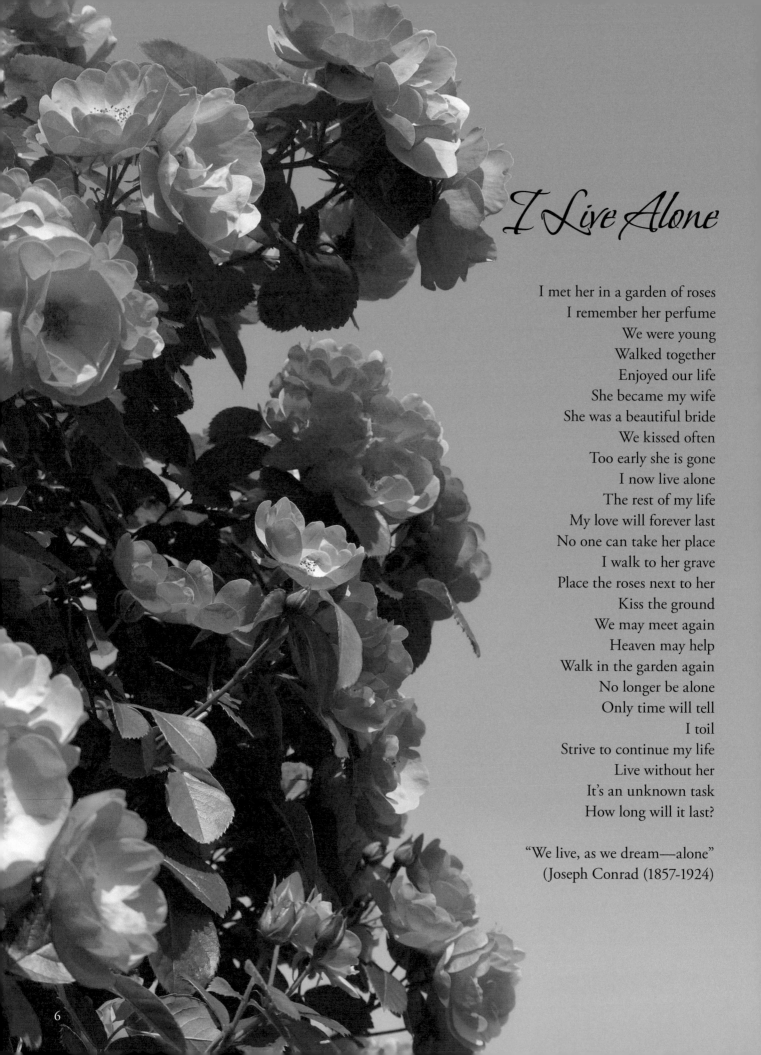

I Live Alone

I met her in a garden of roses
I remember her perfume
We were young
Walked together
Enjoyed our life
She became my wife
She was a beautiful bride
We kissed often
Too early she is gone
I now live alone
The rest of my life
My love will forever last
No one can take her place
I walk to her grave
Place the roses next to her
Kiss the ground
We may meet again
Heaven may help
Walk in the garden again
No longer be alone
Only time will tell
I toil
Strive to continue my life
Live without her
It's an unknown task
How long will it last?

"We live, as we dream—alone"
(Joseph Conrad (1857-1924)

I'm Rich Without Money

I'm rich without money
Three kids and a wife with a magic touch
I'm not handsome
Not as virtuous as I use to be
But she still loves me
I hold the kids
They watch me
They giggle
Touch me
I wonder why
That loving touch is magic
It begins with the touch and streams to the heart

The giggles will soon cease
Replaced with smiles and gentle hugs
The revelation of love changes
The richness remains
The unveiling will alter
The magic is still there
It remains in the heart
Freed with a magic touch

"There are people who have money and people
Who are rich" (Coco Chanel (1883-1970)

Inflamed Love

I can' tell her
Its better if she didn't know
I'm the one who has changed
My love faded
I found someone new
I'm captured
She fulfills my every desire
We met and talked for a long while
She said I have searched for you
I want to see you more
Let me tell you how I feel
Reawaken faded loves Let me
I know our love can last
Life is brief
We live for only a short while
Let us capture the passion
Know it can last
Fulfill our emptiness
Let our lives and love join
Not relive the past
I hope you understand how I feel

"I shall light a candle of understanding
In thine heart, which shall not be put out"

Know loving passion can be real
I have found you
Let us share an inflamed love

Life is Strange

My life is strange
I wish it could be changed
Life moves in unexpected ways
Sometimes it's bright
Sometimes not
We met when we were young
Knew not what our lives would become
Hoped to fulfill our dreams
Dreams are untarnished
Just not real
I loved her
That's still how I feel
She lives deep within me
I wish she would again become real
Walk with me in a new slight
Help me change
Not wipe my life's plate clean

Just wash away what should have been different
We travel through a shifting world
Not knowing what life will bring

"The wave of the future is coming
And there Is no fighting it"
(Anne Morrow Lindbergh (1940)

We always want to be right
That belief is fictional
Failure will always be with us
It's not new
It's just unwelcomed
Realized as we walk in the light
Never young again
Not know how our life will change
Accept the change

Lightning Strikes

When I walked through that door
I saw her once more
I saw her eyes
A lighting bright
I always wanted her
I really didn't know what to do
Walk to her?
Sit beside her?
I saw her smile
She waved
Said stay awhile
It took my breath away
I searched for what to say
Could I tell her how I feel?
That feeling flames when I see her
I hope she knows how I feel

Lightening struck when she held my hand
We walked to the dance floor I
wanted her even more
My hand moved to her waist
She was warm with grace
Her hair remained softly in place
We danced at a slow pace
I touched the dress she wore
I wanted to hold even more
Not on the dance floor
The music stopped
Together we walked out that door

"And on her lover's arm she leant
And around her waist she felt it fold"
(Tennyson (1809-1892)

Longing Place

The bedroom was a wonderous place
I remember her smiling face
Natures pictures on the walls
The trees were tall
Bright green leaves
I remember them all
They were like our love
Shined bright
So did she
There is no place I would rather be
The bedroom remembers it all So do I
The walls glowed a brilliant white
I remember every night
Our loving was like the Spring
It was new
She snuggled close
Held me tight
Then for a reason I can't explain
Something went wrong
She turned away
Pulled the sheets close
Her hands turned cold
So did her heart
The walls turned dark
As did her love
She left the room
I can't remember why
Will this dark room shine again?
I can only wish so
It once was bright with her glowing light
The room is now just a longing place

"Alas, my Love! Ye do me wrong
To cast me of discourteously
And I have loved you so long,
Delighting in your company" (1584)

11

Loose This Sadness

I need to go somewhere
Somewhere I've never been
I don't want to see him again
I did love him so
We met two years ago
We lived together
Made love together
Watched the sun sit and rise
There was a glistening in his eyes
He shared that radiance with me
I thought it would never end
But the brightness dimmed
The passion faded
Our loving ebbed with it
We rarely touched
Two years have been lost
I need to leave this place
Go where I've never been
Remember how to live again
Somewhere to watch the sun sit and rise
Loose this sadness
Somewhere I've never been

"Without hope we live in desire"
(Dante 1265-1321)

"I'll turn over a new leaf"
(Coke (1552-1634)

12

Love Didn't Last

He called me
Wanted to see me
Talk to me
I don't know why
Love was lost long ago
He said I need you so
Our time has passed
Love didn't last
Why call me?
Perhaps I will soon know
He said he loved me
The past was a glorious time
I often wished he were still mine
I wonder what he might see
I'm not what use to be
Hard to explain
My feelings are not the same
I told him so
Want him to know
Love is fleeting
But I remember the feeling
Flaming
The blaze no longer remains
It yet burns
I'll let him see me
It's not what use to be

Loving Moments

I see you
I walk with you
I talk to you
But only in my dreams
My nights are filled when I see you
The dreams vanish when I wake
I wish they endured
I need you
It's you I adore
The dreams I embrace
But I want more
Return to what was before
Loving moments
Times when we walked, talked, made love

Can that return?
Change my dreams to reality?
I don't want to walk alone
I need you beside me
Let me see you
Talk to you
Let my dreams become real
Tell you truly how I feel
Let us dream together
Wake and hold each other
Return to those loving moments

"Lead me from the unreal to the real!
Lead me from darkness to light!. . ."

Stars In Her Eyes

The Pain

I can't take the pain
My love shall remain
But it hurts
It's something you didn't know
I still love you so
Give me that second chance
I know our love can last
Forget the past
Let us begin again
I do believe we can
We will talk
Share our thoughts
Let us try
We have much to lose

Both of us
Please believe me
Forgive me
Help me
It's just you I wish for
Let us try again
We shall celebrate
Know what spirited love can reveal
I love you still
Stop this pain

"Love is an attempt at penetrating another being,
But it can only succeed if the surrender is mutual"
(Outavio Paz 1914)

The Past

I remember the past
Life just doesn't last
The black hair turns grey
My abilities don't remain
Life is a changing game
Sometime liquor takes its place
It helps me forget the past
Sleeping is fleeting
Dreams echo
They are not real
They only recall the past
They are fleeting visions
The mirror reflects the current me
I regret what I see

Making love to you has changed
I wish I were young again
I can only touch you
The passion endures
But it is not the same
I long for a younger me
It will never be
It remains in the past
The dye is cast
Only my dreams remain

"What is past I know, but what
Is for to come I know not"

This Dream Is Killing Me

This dream is killing me
Your image satiates my mind
It's there all the time
Why I just don't know
I can't let it go
It might help if I told you so
We have drifted apart
The dream has taken its place
It doesn't fulfill being with you
Just captures my mind
I can't escape
I've tried
I remain incarcerated
It's slowly killing me
Will you talk to me?
Let me tell you how I feel
I seek freedom
Want to achieve relief
You are real
Distinguishes you from a dream
A key that unlocks despair
Rescues my life
Frees me from the suffering
Help me
The dream Imprisons me
Let me see and talk to you
Tell you how I feel
Remove this dream shackle

"Forget that I remember
And dream that I forget"
(Swinburne (1837-1909)

18

We Live Two Lives

You don't know me
Only a part of me
We all live as two kinds
We change from time-to-time
What you see is open
What you don't see is hidden
Private
How we truly feel
Let me share my private side with you
Something I need to do
You will discover someone new
I never wanted to deceive you
Just please you
Realize there is a private side
Understand me
Know all of me
Let me discover both of you
That private side
The one you hide
Combine our lives
We search for captivating times

'Tomorrow will be a new day"
(Cervantes (1547-1616)

You Are Unkind

You are unkind
I should have known
You were caring
That no longer seems true
Men change I now know
I wish I'd known then

"This was the most unkindness
cut of all"
(Shakespeare)

Men go their own way
That seems true
I know regret we met
Your words are untrue
You just do what you want to do

I'm only a small part of your life
I do wish I could change your mind
Again, be mine.
I'm still here
I could wear that red dress
The one you liked to caress
I remember how it felt
You are so unkind
You wander through life
Care not what life will bring
Men are the same
Don't know that love can last
Surrender the past
I will cast aside that red dress
Just long for that caress

Printed in the United States
by Baker & Taylor Publisher Services